THE
CINEMAS
OF
WEST WALES

ALAN PHILLIPS

First impression: 2017
© Alan Phillips & Y Lolfa Cyf., 2017

Cover design: Y Lolfa
Cover picture: Alan Phillips
Back cover pictures L–R: The Empire Cinema, Milford Haven;
Cross Hands Cinema; Astra Cinema, Pembroke Dock (© W.O. Trevor Mills)

ISBN: 978 1 78461 446 1

Published and printed in Wales
on paper from well-maintained forests by
Y Lolfa Cyf., Talybont, Ceredigion SY24 5HE
e-mail ylolfa@ylolfa.com
website www.ylolfa.com
tel 01970 832 304
fax 832 782

Contents

Introduction

THIS BOOK COVERS the history of cinemas on the west Wales coast, from Barmouth in Gwynedd to Llanelli in Carmarthenshire, as well as cinemas inland. By now most have been demolished or converted to other uses.

In days gone by, in towns and villages, cinemas became landmarks as individual owners competed for the most outstanding structures. They had their own special characteristics and were a central meeting point.

The first purpose-built cinema in the UK opened in 1909. In Wales construction of most cinemas took place in 1910 and 1911, although a number of buildings had been converted into cinemas before that. One of the earliest venues in Wales was the Silvograph Animated Pictures in Rhyl, established in 1906.

Magazines dedicated to film soon followed, giving its readers up-to-date information about the industry and any future releases. *Photoplay*, which was regarded as the ultimate film magazine, was first published in 1911. Others soon followed, like the trade magazines *The Bioscope* and *Kinematograph Weekly*.

In 1939 there were 4,902 cinemas in the UK, most of which remained opened throughout the Second World War. But by the 1950s attendances declined and, as a result, many cinemas closed.

Three important developments happened in the world of the cinema: first, the introduction of sound in the mid 1920s; second, the introduction of colour in the 1930s; and third, CinemaScope (a process in which special lenses are used to compress a wide image into a standard frame) was introduced to cinemas in Wales from 1953 onwards. By 1960 most cinemas had these new elements. It was an expensive change, as prosceniums (the opening separating the stage from the auditorium) had to be widened to accommodate the new wider screens, as well as anamorphic lenses fitted on the projectors.

Cinemas have been a major part of people's lives for a number of years and many have wonderful personal memories of their 'local flicks'. Weekly visits to the local cinema, or 'fleapits' as they were affectionally referred to, were an adventure and often the only form of entertainment available. It was a chance to step back in time or to the future, a chance to forget daily toils and, for an hour or two, be transported to a make-believe world. It was an opportunity to meet friends once or twice a week. Some met their husbands or wives at a film show.

By today the 'local' cinema has more or less completely disappeared and people have to travel a great distance to see a particular film. Admittedly, the cinema multiplexes which have been established in recent decades have their comfortable seating, and offer a choice of at least six or seven different films on their various screens. But they have driven small independent cinemas out of business in the process. However, thankfully, there are still some independent cinemas left in Wales, mostly run by local authorities with the help of volunteers. Over the years the Welsh Government has supported the venues with grants from the European Development Fund which have enabled the cinemas to invest in modern equipment such as digital projectors.

In the early years of cinema, town halls and assembly rooms became the venues for the travelling film shows. Wales had its own film pioneers, such as John Codman, son of the Llandudno pier Punch and Judy man, who travelled throughout north Wales with his magic lantern living picture show. Then there was

Arthur Cheetham who filmed day-to-day scenes throughout the country for the purpose of showing them at venues across most of Wales. He eventually settled in Rhyl and established the first permanent cinema. There was also James Robert Saronie, a photographer from Liverpool who had developed an interest in cinematography and who built up his business during the First World War touring north Wales showing films. He settled in the Prestatyn area, and established cinemas in the town and ran three other cinemas in north Wales. In south and west Wales there was William Haggar, born in Dedham, Essex, but who settled in Aberdare in south Wales. William Haggar was a reputable film-maker. He set up his first Bioscope (travelling cinema) show in Aberavon in 1898 and then toured remote villages throughout south and west Wales with it. In 1910 he opened his first purpose-built cinema in Aberdare; the Coliseum was later renamed Haggar's Electric Palace. Other cinemas of his followed in Llanelli, Pontarddulais, Neath, Mountain Ash and Pembroke.

The travelling film showmen contributed a great deal in introducing moving pictures to the masses. The Dooner family,

Haggar's Bioscope

A Bioscope Electric Cinema (© Hollycombe Steam Museum)

Crecraft, Cecil Hepworth, Sidney White's Electric Coliseum Bioscope, Wadbrook and Haggar regularly visited the various annual funfairs throughout south and west Wales.

The early cinemas were very primitive – the screen was usually a white canvas sheet or even a white painted wall, while the projector was located at the back of the auditorium. However, after the Cinematograph Act of 1909/10, halls had to obtain a licence to operate as a cinema. The layout of halls had to change, projector boxes had to be away from the audience, preferably in a fire resistant enclosure. One must remember film stock was made from nitrate, and that was highly flammable.

As a result several halls failed the stringent safety rules and ceased operating as cinemas. Others flourished and drew greater audiences as a consequence. Several cinemas with more lavish auditoriums were built before the First World War, but the most elaborate ones were built in the 1920s and 1930s.

Over the years great strides were made in cinematography, with nitrate film replaced by safety film. The silent projectors

Wadbrook's Royal Electrograph often visited south Wales's fairgrounds

were replaced by Sound-on-disc and eventually by a proper sound system. Colour films were introduced and, as noted, CinemaScope in 1953. New projectors emerged, replacing the hand cranking machines of the early 1900s and the pre-1930s, equipment which showed films with stereophonic sound. Some cinemas used 70 mm film equipment which gave the filmgoer a new experience. Today, in most cinemas, the 35 mm film projectors have been replaced by Sony 4K digital projectors, which are capable of showing not only feature films but also live performances of shows, operas, ballets and musicals direct from London's West End.

By the 1960s, with the advent of television and increased running costs, cinema attendances declined and several went into financial difficulty. Some cinemas / theatres were converted into bingo halls or were used for other uses, such as supermarkets, or eventually demolished. Today several cinemas have been taken over by J.D. Wetherspoon pubs, and they have retained the décor to give us a glimpse of their former glory days.

A pre-1900 projector

A Kalee 8 with Sound-on-disc equipment

A Kalee 11 projector became standard equipment in most cinemas

A typical auditorium in the 1950s

Aberaeron, Ceredigion

The seaside resort town of Aberaeron is situated between Aberystwyth and Cardigan on the shore of Cardigan Bay. Since the 1800s it has grown from a coastal village to a small town popular with holidaymakers. Nowadays it is renowned for its brightly painted houses.

The **Palace Cinema** in Market Street was the first cinema in the town. It was issued with a cinematography licence in 1915. Initially it was equipped with a hand-crank Kalee projector but that was replaced by a motorised version. The cinema was never adapted for sound. The seats were basic wooden benches with a seating capacity for 200 patrons. The Palace Cinema ran nightly film shows from Monday to Friday with two changes of programme per week. The Palace ceased to be a cinema in 1928/9 and closed a year later. Today the building is a retail outlet but the cinema frontage remains.

The **Memorial Hall** on South Road was built with donations collected by local people in memory of those who died in the First World War. The hall was opened on 1 April 1925. It had a reasonably-sized stage with dressing rooms, and the projector box was suspended from the ceiling over the entrance to the hall. Seating capacity was 399. The hall had a proscenium of 22 feet and a screen size of 18 x 12 feet. In 1933 the cinema was licensed to Mr Griffith Rees and was fitted with the Morrison sound system. The cinema presented one show weekly throughout the 1930s. In 1935 the proprietor was listed as Mr M. Jones and was part of the Western Cinema Circuit. In 1948 BTH Supa Cinema projectors and sound system had been installed, and the proprietor was Mr David C. Lloyd.

By 1943 the cinema showed a nightly performance, Monday to Friday, with two shows on a Saturday. However, with the advent of television, only one film per month was transmitted in 1954. Today the hall has been renovated to a high standard and

The Memorial Hall during its cinema days

The interior of the multifunction hall nowadays

The hall as it is today

is used for various community events, including the occasional film showing.

Aberdovey, Gwynedd

Aberdovey (Aberdyfi in Welsh) is situated on the north side of the Dyfi estuary. It grew in the 18th century to become an important harbour and shipbuilding centre. Today it's a popular tourist destination.

The **Picture House** on the A493 was an ex-Army wooden building, erected in 1920 as a community hall for the town. Initially called the **Pavilion**, it was used for concerts and as a base for the local drama society. By the 1940s the building was in a poor state of repairs and had to be replaced. After the Second World War it was known as the **Pavilion Cinema**. Proprietor of the cinema until its closure in 1954 was Mr H.T. Parkes. The

The Picture House / Pavilion Cinema in Aberdovey

It has been refurbished and is now called Neuadd Dyfi

venue had a proscenium of 26 feet and a stage depth of 23 feet, and two dressing rooms. The auditorium had a seating capacity in 1947 for 395, but by 1954 that had been reduced to 323 seats. Initially the cinema was equipped with Emophone Klang equipment but by 1954 Ziess Ikon Ernemann equipment was used. The Pavilion Cinema showed one performance nightly, apart from on Saturdays when it was used for local events. In 2000 the hall was completely refurbished and renamed Neuadd Dyfi. It is a multifunction hall with 232 seats (153 stackable type) and is capable of showing films from a suspended digital projector.

Aberystwyth, Ceredigion
Aberystwyth is a major resort and university town on Cardigan Bay and has had several cinemas over the years.

One of the earliest cinemas in the town was the **Rink Cinema / Picture Theatre** on the junction of Portland Street and Queens Square. Built as a roller-skating rink in 1880, it was converted into a theatre in the 1890s. It was taken over in 1899 by Fred E. Young, a keen supporter of cinema as a means of entertainment. Later, Solomon Andrews staged an exhibition featuring Edison's new machine for projecting motion pictures using celluloid film at the theatre. The Rink Cinema closed in 1908 but the building reopened in 1913 when Mr C. Fear installed silent movie projectors. But a year later the cinema closed once more and remained shut throughout the First World War. In 1919 it was reopened by Mr E.J. Evans of Llanelli who refurbished the 600-seat cinema. There would now be continuous performances, Monday to Saturday, with at least three film changes per week. The cinema closed again in 1921 and the building was demolished in 1923.

Cheetham's Picture Palace and Electric Theatre, at the

Eastgate end of Market Street, was Aberystwyth's first purpose-built cinema. It was opened in 1911 by Gus A. Cheetham, son of the film pioneer Arthur Cheetham. As noted already, Arthur Cheetham of Rhyl's Silvograph Animated Pictures fame began making his own moving pictures and toured extensively all over Wales. He visited Aberystwyth several times and eventually decided to build a cinema there. The Picture Palace, or the **Palladium** as it was also known, continued to show films throughout the First World War. Modest refurbishment took place in 1919 with the installation of new seating for 300 people as well as showing more recent films. Talking pictures were introduced in 1927, using a Sound-on-disc machine. In 1931 the Palladium had British Thompson-Houston (BTH) cinema projectors and sound system. As Aberystwyth depended on seasonal trade, attendances fell and the Palladium closed its doors in 1934 and was demolished soon afterwards. Today the site is occupied by the Pantyfedwen offices.

The **Pier Theatre**, at the front of Aberystwyth's Royal Pier, was converted to a cinema in 1912, but Fred E. Young showed moving pictures of Prime Minister William Gladstone's funeral

Aberystwyth Royal Pier had a cinema

there on an Edison machine in 1900. The 1,000-seat auditorium had a 40-foot-wide proscenium large enough for the biggest choirs. However, the cinema seating was reduced to 615 so that everyone could have a clear view of the 24-foot-wide screen. The **Pier Pavilion**, as it eventually became known, was converted to sound in 1922 with the installation of Electrochord, then the AWH sound system, but later it was changed to the RCA Photophone system. In January 1938 the pier was damaged by a storm and, after repairs, the cinema seating was reduced yet again. The Pier Pavilion's cinema proprietor in 1947 was Mr M.E. Binet. During the summer months there were two shows nightly, while during the winter just one show per night. In 1961 the cinema and part of the pier was severely damaged by a fire; however, even after repairs and repainting the cinema discontinued.

Another of Aberystwyth's cinemas was the **Imperial Cinema** on Bath Street. In 1931 the proprietor was Mr W.J. Evans. Films were shown nightly, Monday to Saturday. By the late 1930s it was known as the **Forum Cinema** and had a seating capacity of 496 and a proscenium width of 35 feet. The Forum Cinema ceased operating throughout the Second World War and was used by Navy, Army, Air Force Institute military personnel based around the town instead.

Aberystwyth's other cinemas were the **Conway** and the **Celtic** on Bath Street. The Conway, formerly known as the Little Theatre, was converted from the ladies' public baths which closed on the site in 1946. It was adapted into a cinema in 1961 and had a specially constructed projector box. It already had a small stage and dressing room when it was a theatre. Initially the cinema was equipped with Kalee projectors, but these were replaced in 1966 with BTH Supa Cinema projectors and sound system.

The **Celtic Cinema** next door dates back to pre-1930, the

The Celtic Cinema on Bath Street
(© Ceredigion Archives)

The Conway Cinema was next door to the Celtic Cinema

The Conway and Celtic shared the same entrance which is to the left in this photograph, near the sign

proprietor being Mr H.H. Barker. The 434-seat cinema had a proscenium width of 35 feet and was equipped with RCA sound system. In 1964 it was equipped with Ross G.C.3 projectors and Ross Streemlite Arc Lamps.

Both cinemas showed nightly performances Monday to Friday, with two shows on Saturdays. Normally there were two film changes per week. Entrance to both cinemas was via a building constructed between the two. The Conway and the Celtic cinemas closed in the early 1970s and were demolished in 1975 to make room for the Commodore Cinema.

The **Commodore Cinema**, Bath Street, was opened in 1978. The 410-seat single screen cinema is independently owned and is one of the cheapest cinemas to visit in Wales. Initially equipped with 35 mm projectors, it is now equipped with digital projectors and full Dolby SR surround sound capable of showing 3D films.

Phillips Coliseum Theatre, built by stonemason David

The Commodore Cinema in 1977. It was built on the site of the Conway and Celtic cinemas.

(© Ceredigion Archives)

The Commodore Cinema as it is today

23

The interior of the Coliseum Theatre in its heyday
(© Ceredigion Archives)

Another image of the Coliseum interior from the upper gallery

The Coliseum was turned into a museum

The street view of the Coliseum Theatre

Phillips, was opened as an entertainment hall in 1905, with an arcade, offices and a stable on the ground floor. Over the years some 5,000 events were held at the theatre, ranging from concerts to variety shows including, one year, the National Eisteddfod of Wales. The theatre had a 27-foot proscenium, with a stage width of 25 feet and depth of 14 feet. There were two dressing rooms but other rooms could be used if required. Initially, the seating capacity was 1,400, but it was reduced to 800 later. The auditorium had two horseshoe-shaped balconies, with three rows of seats extending down to the proscenium. In 1932 the theatre was converted into a cinema, with seating capacity reduced to 650 and the building equipped with British Acoustic sound system. During the 1950s new seating was installed in the dress circle, balcony and stalls. CinemaScope was introduced in 1955. Mr and Mrs Gale continued as proprietors until its closure in May 1976. Aberystwyth had a large number of cinemas and it was inevitable that some would close with the advent of television and a decline in cinema attendance. The Coliseum Cinema was later taken over by Cardiganshire County Council and turned into a museum. The theatre's layout was kept intact, depicting the building's former glory.

The **Kings Hall**, built in the Art Deco style in 1933, was opened on 27 June 1934. It had a large auditorium, balcony and stage capable of putting on the most lavish of productions, with a projector box and ample dressing rooms. Built as an entertainment centre for the town, it held weekly dances and was also a venue for visiting pop group concerts and variety shows. During the summer season films were shown between the live events. By the 1980s the hall had deteriorated and was in need of extensive repairs. There was no finance available, so the venue closed and was demolished in 1989 with apartments built on the site.

The **Elysium Cinema** (Elysium Grove) on Terrace Road was

The Kings Hall was the town's main venue for live performances and it also showed films

Its impressive auditorium

It was situated in a prominent position on the promenade

The site of the Kings Hall today

a wooden 200-seat theatre converted to show films in 1921. It continued to show silent films, accompanied by a pianist, until it closed in 1926.

The **Aberystwyth Arts Centre** is a cultural and entertainment venue on Aberystwyth University's campus. The centre comprises a concert hall, theatre, studio and a 125-seat cinema equipped with a Digital HD projector capable of showing 3D films with Dolby Stereo. The Arts Centre was opened in phases, with the cinema opening in 2000. At least two different films are shown weekly.

Ammanford, Carmarthenshire

Ammanford (Rhydaman in Welsh) is a town which lies in a former coal mining area. It is now the main shopping centre for the Amman valley.

Sidney White frequently visited the town with his travelling film shows in the early 1900s. A temporary cinema was set up in a marquee built on land behind the arcade just off Wind Street.

The first purpose-built Bioscope cinema was John R. Poole's on Margaret Street in 1910. **Poole's Pictorium** seated 650 people on wooden benches. It showed silent films until it closed in the late 1920s. In 1936 the building was bought by the James Bus Company and was demolished. Today houses have been built on the site.

The **Palace Cinema** was built adjacent to the arcade on College Street in 1912 by local man Mr Evan Evans. It had a very distinguished redbrick frontage. Originally known as **White's Palace** (in reference to Sidney White's earlier visits), the cinema had a reasonably-sized stage and was often used as a musical hall, especially during the First World War. The 600-seat auditorium was enlarged in the 1920s, with alterations to the balcony and new seating increasing capacity to 895. The Palace was acquired by the South Wales Cinema chain. It had a Melotone sound system in 1931 (but changed to a Western Electric sound system in 1946). In March 1937 the Palace was taken over by the Union Cinemas chain but, by October 1937, the company had been absorbed into the Associated British Cinemas (ABC) group. With the introduction of CinemaScope in 1954, the proscenium was widened from 20 feet to 35 feet, and seating reduced to 841. On 30 September 1956, ABC sold the cinema to an independent operator who continued to run it until its final closure when the building was badly damaged by a fire on 4 June 1977. The gutted building was only demolished in July 1981 and, at the time of writing, the site is a car park.

The **Miners' Welfare Hall and Institute** on Wind Street, designed by Owen J. Parry and opened in October 1932, was built as an entertainment centre for variety concerts and for showing films. The building had a redbrick frontage with ornate terracotta columns. The balcony had 220 seats, with a further 540 seats on ground level. The proscenium was 20 feet wide and the stage 14 feet deep. There were two reasonably-sized dressing rooms. The hall was equipped with BTH cinema projectors and sound system and the first projectionist was Mr D. Brin Daniel. When not in use for live performances, the hall was used for one film show per night with two changes of programme a week. Like the Palace Cinema, the Miners' Institute continued to show films throughout the Second World War. In the mid 1950s CinemaScope was installed but, by the end of the decade, audiences had declined in number and the Miners' Institute concentrated on live performances. It ceased showing films altogether by the mid 1970s. Over the next 20 years the hall fell into a state of disrepair and eventually closed. However, in 1994, CADW listed the structure Grade II, and in 2000 the hall was refurbished as a multipurpose venue (with cinema facilities available) with 120 seats.

The Miners' Institute has always been a venue for entertainment

The interior of the Miners' Institute before redevelopment

31

Barmouth, Gwynedd

Barmouth (Abermaw or Y Bermo in Welsh) is situated on the estuary of the River Mawddach. The town grew as a result of the shipbuilding industry of the 19th century. Nowadays it is a popular seaside resort.

The **New White Cinema**, St Anne's Square, dates back to 1923. The 375-seat cinema had a proscenium width of 18 feet. As the building had a corrugated roof, on wet days and nights the sound had to be increased to drown out the noise of the rain! Continuous performances occurred during the summer months but, by 1950, there was only one performance daily with matinées on Wednesdays and Saturdays. The cinema was equipped with Gyrotone sound system and CinemaScope was introduced in 1954. At that time the proprietor was Mr D.E. Davies. With cinema attendance in decline, it closed towards the end of the 1950s.

Barmouth's other cinema was the **Pavilion** on the promenade. This dates back to the early 1920s, and a dance

The Pavilion Cinema on Barmouth promenade

hall was attached to the 650-seat cinema. With the advent of talkies, an AWH sound system was installed. The Pavilion proscenium was 23 feet wide and the stage 15 feet deep. In 1931 there was one show nightly during the winter months. Just like the New White Cinema, it continued showing films throughout the Second World War. CinemaScope was installed in the mid 1950s but by the 1960s attendances declined and it was forced to close.

In the early 1950s work began on converting the 1890 English Congregational Chapel in Jubilee Road into a community centre. As a result the 237-seat **Dragon Theatre (Theatr y Ddraig)** opened on 30 October 1959. It had a stage measuring 25 x 25 feet, with its associate equipment used constantly by local drama groups. During phase one of a redevelopment plan in 1970s, an extension was built at the rear and a new foyer at the side. The second phase of the

The Dragon Theatre is a multifunction hall

The Dragon Theatre's auditorium

development in 2000 was financed by the Welsh European Funding Office and Gwynedd County Council's Regeneration Fund. The auditorium was redeveloped and new seating and gold curtains added. A digital projector was installed with a roll-down screen. Seating capacity was reduced to 186 in the stalls, balcony and the two boxes.

Borth, Ceredigion

Borth is a small coastal village, some seven miles north of Aberystwyth. Nowadays it is a popular holiday resort with many caravan and camping sites. It is one of the filming locations for the *Hinterland* television series.

The earliest film exploits in the village was a visiting cinema company in the 1950s. But, in 2014, Gerlan Chapel, which was built in 1877, was bought by film enthusiasts Peter Fleming and Grug Morris for conversion into a boutique cinema, theatre and restaurant. The **Libanus 1877 Cinema**, which opened in early 2017 to mark the building's 140th year, has a single screen, a small stage and eventually apartments will be built at the rear. Two-thirds of the interior is utilised for the cinema/theatre, with luxurious seating and attached tables for meals. It is equipped with digital projectors providing satellite links to live shows from London.

Burry Port, Carmarthenshire

Burry Port (Porth Tywyn in Welsh) is around five miles from Llanelli. It was a farming and fishing village before the Industrial Revolution. Amelia Earhart landed her plane near Burry Port harbour after her solo flight across the Atlantic on 17 June 1928.

Cinema came to Burry Port in the early 1900s when Arthur Cheetham showed his own short films. They included a film of William 'Buffalo Bill' Cody's visit to Rhyl in 1903. William Haggar also visited the town, showing his film of a train arriving and departing from Burry Port railway station. Other film enthusiasts also visited the area with their Bioscope film shows.

The first cinema was on the site of the English Baptist Chapel on Stepney Road. The corrugated building was vacated as a chapel in 1913 and then converted into a cinema. It showed continuous film shows in 1913 but seems to have ceased operating by the outbreak of the First World War. In the 1920s the building was renovated, with pews removed and individual seats fitted. A projection box equipped with Kalee projectors was installed. In 1931 the proprietor was Thomas Williams who was also involved with several other cinemas in the area. Known as the **Stepney Cinema**, it had seating for 118 and was demolished in 1987.

Other cinemas, which appeared in newspaper advertisements of the time, included ones located in the Parish Hall, Memorial Hall and Burry Port Cinema, but cinema names often changed and these could be one and the same.

Twm's Cinema, as it was affectionately called, was a corrugated iron-built building from the 1920s. Today a school, Burry Port's Ysgol Glan-y-môr, occupies the site and the pupils have constructed a garden in memory of Twm's Cinema.

The **Adelphi Cinema**, Seaview Terrace, overlooking the harbour, was a luxurious cinema which opened in October 1937. It was equipped with a large stage, with dressing rooms at the rear. As well as showing films and plays, concerts and musicals were often performed. The owner was Mr Labor Dennis who often greeted people as they entered the venue. The 900-seat cinema had BTH cinema projectors and sound system. In 1947 the cinema was taken over by Mr Thomas Williams. In the early 1950s it was granted a bingo licence, and this activity was held a few days each week. In 1954 it was run by the Burry

The Adelphi Cinema opened in 1937

Port Cinema Ltd. CinemaScope was installed in 1955. With the closure of the nearby RAF airfield at Pembrey and the decline in cinema attendance, it closed in May 1959 and was demolished in 1972/3 to make way for a car park.

Cardigan, Ceredigion

Cardigan (Aberteifi in Welsh) developed around the Norman castle situated at the mouth of the River Teifi. Location of the first National Eisteddfod in 1176, the market town is full of interesting historical buildings and nowadays is a popular shopping centre.

Cinema in Cardigan can be traced back to the Bioscope shows which were shown during the visits of fairgrounds.

Cardigan's one and only cinema, the **Pavilion**, was officially opened on 6 November 1912 by the then mayor Mr Ivor Evans. The 800-seat cinema was owned by the Cardigan Pavilion Company Ltd and was located at Napier Gardens. The building was made of corrugated iron walls lined with wooden panelling. The Pavilion was equipped with a small stage and a proscenium width of 24 feet. The silent films shown were accompanied by a piano player. Initially the Pavilion only staged three shows a week, with one matinée, but increased to nightly shows, with additional screenings during the summer months. For example, on 12 September 1913, the film *Territorials* was shown to a packed audience, much of which featured the Cardigan Company of Rifle Volunteers at Haverfordwest. The Pavilion hit the headlines on 9 February 1916 by showing the controversial Sidney Olcott film, *From the Manger to the Cross* (1912), which had been banned by the Church. In 1931 BTH cinema projectors and a Western Electric sound system was installed. During the Second World War the cinema continued to operate. In 1945 it was taken over by the Cardigan Cinema Company. In 1955 CinemaScope was introduced which gave the cinema a screen width of 24 feet, but

The Pavilion Cinema dates back to 1912

(© E.R. Williams)

seating was, however, reduced to 554. For the next few years the Pavilion continued to operate under different owners. In the 1960s the auditorium was redecorated; several rows towards the front were removed, reducing the seating capacity to 350. By the end of the 1970s it had been taken over by Fry's Entertainments of Tenby. On 22 November 1984 the Pavilion closed as a cinema. The building was used as a bingo hall and, later, in 1991, as a snooker hall; that eventually closing too. It was demolished on 11 April 1996. Nowadays the site is occupied by bungalows.

Theatr Mwldan, Bath House Road, is a £7 million entertainment complex development. It has three fully digital screens, with one capable of showing 3D films. Mwldan 1 is a 146-seat cinema; Mwldan 2 is a 249-seat cinema/theatre which was refurbished and extended in 2004; and Mwldan 3 a 101-seat luxury cinema with alfresco seating, added in 2012. In 2014 a café, shop and a number of other rooms were added for various functions. Mwldan 3 is also often used for live events, and showing performances from London theatres via a satellite link.

The entrance to Theatr Mwldan

Theatr Mwldan's auditorium

The stage/screen area in one of the theatres

40

Carmarthen, Carmarthenshire

Carmarthen (Caerfyrddin in Welsh) dates back to Roman times and nowadays is an important shopping centre for the population of west Wales.

Carmarthen's first taste of cinematography was courtesy of travelling fairground pioneers such as William Haggar, Wadbrook, Crecraft and Pat Collins who regularly visited the annual funfairs. Harry and Fred Poole's Myriorama (travelling panorama shows) also visited the town on several occasions. These early Bioscope shows continued until 1905.

In August 1910 the **Market Cinema** advertised Wadbrook's Royal Picture & Variety Company showing films including *The Beggar's Gratitude* (1909) together with live variety acts at the Market Hall. No further film showings took place and it seems this was a one-off.

The first building adopted as a cinema was the **Assembly Rooms** on King Street which opened on 21 November 1854. Originally meant for the purpose of dancing, lectures and concerts, the 64 x 34-foot venue could hold nearly 600 people. Poole's Myriorama and Myriograph were regularly shown from 1899 until 1905. For the next few years William Haggar also visited the Assembly Rooms on a regular basis with his film shows. On 1 April 1918 the Assembly Rooms became known as the **Lyric**, providing the town with a permanent cinema and concert venue.

The manager of the Lyric at the time was Mr Tom Barger of the Palace Cinema, Pembroke Dock. The first films shown at the venue were a Gaumont comedy, *The War Office Budget* and *Rasputin* (1928). Two shows per day were the norm, with two changes of programme per week. Western Electric sound was introduced in 1930 when the film *Sonny Boy* (1928), with Al Jolson singing the title song, was shown. In March 1931 the Lyric

The Assembly Rooms opened on 21 November 1854 for lectures and entertainment
(© Carmarthen Library)

The Lyric Cinema, originally known as the Assembly Rooms

42

closed for extensive alterations: the backstage was extended, a café added and the proscenium width was increased to 20 feet. It reopened on 4 April 1931 after just two weeks, under new manager Mr W.E. Morgan.

On land adjacent to the Lyric a new auditorium was built in the Art Deco style. This was called the **New Lyric**, and had seating capacity for 900 people in the stalls and circle, but this was reduced to 800 with the introduction of CinemaScope in the 1950s. It had a 36-foot proscenium, with a large stage and fly tower where scenery could be suspended. It opened on 6 August 1936 with the film *Heart's Desire* (1935) starring Richard Tauber. The sound system was moved from the old building. The cinema continued to operate more or less throughout the Second World War, with two shows each evening and matinées on Wednesdays and Saturdays. Mr B.A. Harrack took over control of the New Lyric in the 1970s until its closure in August 1983. The building

Today the New Lyric stages live shows mostly

lay empty until it was taken over by the local council in 1986 which made some renovations to the building and stage area. Since 1987 the New Lyric has put on various live shows as well as films occasionally. Nowadays the theatre is the venue for live performances and concerts.

Built in 1909 and opened a year later by the mayor of Carmarthen, the **Rink** on Station Road was a brick and corrugated iron structure with wooden panelling. As roller-skating became less popular, other forms of entertainment were considered for the venue. It was opened as a cinema on 21 December 1911 and is accredited as the town's first proper cinema. Initially known as the **Rink Picture House** and later as the **Rink Picturedrome**, it had seating capacity for 700 people and a small stage. In 1915 it was leased to Mr W.T. Rogers who remained its manager until 1917. By then there were three other cinemas in the town and the Rink cinema closed, reverting back to being a skating rink once more.

Vint's Electric Palace Cinema on Blue Street was designed by Ernest Collier and opened on 1 April 1912. The 600-seat

venue was built as a cinema / variety theatre. Initially, live variety shows and touring drama groups performed at the Palace and film shows were included between the live events. Owner Leon Vint was the proprietor of some 14 similar halls in the Midlands and south Wales. In February 1914 the theatre closed, but

The Empire Cinema site on Blue Street nowadays

was taken over by Mr Horace W. Bolton and reopened as the **Empire Cinema**. Throughout the First World War it continued to stage productions by national touring companies as well as popular films of the times like *The Jockey of Death* (1915), *Life's Highway* (1915), *Married to a German Spy* (1915) and other war films that were produced. In the early 1920s the proprietor of the Empire was Tom Barger; then Norman Barger took over in 1930. During that period there was one show nightly with two film changes per week. In March 1931 the cinema closed for refurbishment: the fitting of new seating, rewiring the building, adding extra lights and the installation of Imperial sound system. It reopened at the end of the month with 884 seats. In 1935 the venue closed again and was leased to Mr P.F.J. Bosisto who reopened it as a cinema / variety theatre. In 1936 the Empire was taken over by the Capitol Cinema Company but closed in 1938 and was converted into a garage in 1947. Nowadays it is divided into two retail outlets.

Up until the 1930s all of Carmarthen's cinema venues had been converted from other uses. The **Capitol Cinema** on John Street was built as a 'super-cinema' from the outset. Local company Capitol (Carmarthen) Ltd built it on the site of an old tannery in 1929. The proprietors were Messrs H.E. Weight and G.B. Baker. Western Electric sound system was installed prior to opening in August 1930. The stalls and two-tier balconies could accommodate nearly 1,000 people. *The Desert Song* (1929) starring John Boles, Carlotta King and Louise Fazenda was the opening film. The Capitol was equipped with a reasonably-sized stage capable of hosting the largest of choirs or productions. Throughout the Second World War the Capitol admission prices remained the same. By 1947 the seating capacity had been reduced to 984 due to the removal of damaged seating. The post-war period brought an increase in pricing, especially in the higher circle seats. In 1955 CinemaScope was installed at the Capitol,

The Capitol was once one of town's premier cinemas

Nowadays the Capitol building is in a sorry state

46

necessitating the fitting of a new large screen (44 feet in width by 20 feet). With the decline in cinema attendances, bingo was introduced in the 1960s. By 1969 the Capitol had its own social club and put on regular cabaret shows. This enterprise didn't last long and the venue closed, with the stalls area converted into a snooker hall. However, by 1996, it too closed and the Capitol remained empty until it became a retail store and health club.

Part of Carmarthen's recent redevelopment has included the **Apollo** cinema chain building a multiplex on the St Catherine's Walk site. It was the first all-digital purpose-built cinema in Wales. Equipped with Sony 4K digital projectors, it can show 3D films. The multiplex consists of six screens: Screen 1 with seating capacity for 334; Screen 2 – 208 seats; Screen 3 – 103 seats; Screen 4 – 101 seats; Screen 5 – 64 seats; and Screen 6 with 94 seats. The Apollo group was taken over by Vue Cinemas in January 2013 and the Carmarthen multiplex changed its name to **Vue** soon afterwards.

With the coming of the Apollo cinema complex, the town has more cinema screens than ever before

(© EWA design company)

The lavish interior of the Apollo cinema complex
(© EWA design company)

The Apollo cinema chain was taken over by the Vue Cinema group in 2013

Cross Hands, Carmarthenshire

Cross Hands is a village situated some 12 miles from Carmarthen.

The **Public Hall** on Carmarthen Road was built in 1906, and its upkeep largely funded by miners' contributions. The rear of the building was extended in 1920 and again in 1932. It once had a French-inspired façade, with the auditorium ceiling being of Italian design. Seating capacity was well over 300 in the stalls and balcony. It showed nightly cinema performances on Mondays, Tuesdays and Fridays, with the remaining nights devoted to other functions. It was initially equipped with Kalee projectors and a Western Electric sound system, but that was replaced by a single Cinemeccanica Victoria 5 CX20H system which in turn was replaced by a Barco/Kinton digital system after refurbishment. In 1984 the venue closed due to its state of disrepair. In 1991 finance was acquired to repair and refurbish the hall and it was reopened on 26 April 1996. It is now run by a team of dedicated volunteers and shows films three times a week.

Cross Hands Public Hall (right) in 1906

The Public Hall in 1983 prior to renovation

Cross Hands cinema today

The cinema's auditorium
(© Cross Hands cinema)

Another view of the auditorium

51

The stage area of Cross Hands cinema
(© Cross Hands cinema)

Today the cinema shows up-to-date films

The **Capitol Cinema** on Llandeilo Road was first listed in the *Kinematograph Year Book* in 1931 with Mr Chris Evans as its proprietor. The 650-seat cinema was equipped with the Sound-on-disc system. The Capitol was built as a cinema/variety venue with a 22-foot proscenium, stage depth of 14 feet, and six dressing rooms. In 1937 brothers Chris and Jack Evans ran the cinema. RCA equipment was installed in 1942 to match the superior sound system in the Public Hall. By 1954 Capitol Cinema (Cross Hands) Ltd was its owner. CinemaScope was fitted in the mid 1950s which gave a screen size of 20 x 14 feet but the seating was reduced to 400. The cinema closed soon afterwards in 1956, and it was later converted into a factory manufacturing television sets. In June 1975 the building was destroyed by fire and was demolished.

Dolgellau, Gwynedd

Dolgellau is a market town in Gwynedd and was the county town of Merionethshire until 1974. Tourism is an important contributor to the local economy nowadays.

The **Cosy Cinema** was part of E.H. James's chain which had cinemas in Llanrwst, Llanfairfechan and Menai Bridge in north Wales. The cinema was located in the Assembly Rooms (built in 1870) on Eldon Square. Over the years this stone-built building has been a town hall, a dance hall, a grain store (during both world wars) and a cinema. In 1930 E.H. James acquired a licence to run a cinema in the gallery which had been built in the late 1920s. Information is rather sketchy, as the venue is not mentioned in *Kinematograph Year Books*, but it is believed, according to local reports, that a nightly film was shown. The Cosy Cinema continued operating until 1947, except for a period during the Second World War. Today the building is known as the Idris Hall, and it is a community venue.

The Cosy Cinema (right)

Nowadays the building has been converted for other uses

Dolgellau's other cinema was the **Plaza** and it belonged to Guy Baker of Paramount Picture Theatres in Welshpool. The Plaza on Barmouth Road was a purpose-built cinema / theatre built in 1944 and capable of holding 500 people. Seating was on one level and it had a reasonably-sized stage with two dressing rooms. Access to the projection box was via steps on the outside of the building. Initially it was equipped with AWH sound system but changed to British Acoustic in 1966. Films were shown nightly, Monday to Friday, and then twice on Saturdays. At first there was a programme change three times a week. CinemaScope was introduced in the mid 1950s. With the death of Guy Baker in 1983, the Paramount Picture Theatres company ceased trading and most of the chain's cinemas closed, including the Plaza in 1984. No buyer could be found and the building was demolished. Today a new police station has been built on the site.

Fishguard, Pembrokeshire

The origins of Fishguard (Abergwaun in Welsh) can be traced back to Viking times when it was a Norse trading post. However, it was after the Norman Conquest that the town grew. It is divided into two parts: Fishguard and Lower Fishguard, which is a small fishing hamlet. The Fishguard area became famous during the French invasion of 1797. The surrender document of the Battle of Fishguard was signed in the Royal Oak Inn on the town square.

In 1878 a Temperance Hall was built on West Street for private education and recreation. In 1900 major renovation of the building took place, with the installation of a stage and associate equipment. Later, Bioscope films, such as *The Old Chorister* (1904) and *Down on the Farm* (1920), were shown. The hall also continued to host live performances from local and touring groups.

In 1926 the Temperance Hall was converted into a cinema. A projection box was built over the entrance to the hall, and the wooden benches were replaced by 450 tip-up seats. Initially only silent films were shown but sound was soon introduced. By 1931 the cinema was equipped with Kalee projectors and a Western Electric sound system. Known just as the **Cinema**, it was owned by the Williams family. It showed one performance nightly and two on Wednesdays and Saturdays; there were two film changes a week. It continued operating for most of the Second World War. CinemaScope was introduced in 1955, and this reduced seating capacity to 252.

In 1980 the cinema was taken over by the local council who refurbished the building and renamed it the **Studio Cinema**. During a further 1990 refurbishment, the auditorium was completely transformed, with new projectors, Dolby Sound, new curtains and 180 new seats installed. The remodelled venue was renamed **Theatr Gwaun**. Pembrokeshire County Council was unable to sustain financial support for the theatre and closure was imminent until local supporters came up with a valid business plan to keep the theatre open. Today it is run by the Friends of Theatr Gwaun and up-to-date films are shown on a newly-installed Sony 4K digital projector.

The Studio Cinema was originally the Temperance Hall
(© Fishguard History)

The side view of the Studio Cinema

The Studio Cinema / Theatr Gwaun as it is today

The cinema's auditorium
(© Studio Cinema / Theatr Gwaun)

The renovated auditorium of Theatr Gwaun

Haverfordwest, Pembrokeshire

Haverfordwest (Hwlffordd in Welsh) is the county town of Pembrokeshire and is situated on the River Cleddau. Its origins can be dated back to the late 11th century.

Strolling players or travelling theatre groups often visited the town in the 18th century, performing in pubs, halls and even in the open air. The first official venue for such events was the Town Hall in 1769, but that was later replaced by the Masonic Hall in Picton Place which opened in 1872. The town's first encounter with moving pictures was early in the 1900s when various showmen visited the annual Portfield fair, such as William Haggar and his Royal Electric Bioscope, the Dooner family, Crecraft, Wadbrook, Cecil Hepworth and Sidney White's Electric Coliseum Bioscope. In 1909 there were five Bioscope shows at the Portfield fair but, after the Cinematograph Act of that year, only three attended the fair in future years.

White's Palace / New Palace Cinema on Upper Market Street was initially the town's Corn Market and was owned by Sidney White. The theatre had a small stage and could hold about 1,000 people seated on long wooden benches. It opened on 28 July 1913 with the film *Zuma, Queen of the Gipsies* (1913) accompanied by a live variety show. The live performances proved to be more popular than the film shows, so the film slots were reduced! In 1916 Sidney White sold the New Palace to a local syndicate, Cinema Palace Syndicate. Mr Arthur Williams became resident manager. Stage facilities were improved, more lights and curtains added, and the seating capacity reduced to 800 with the installation of tip-up seats. The cinema / variety arrangements continued throughout the First World War but, by 1920, the New Palace was advertised as having only one show nightly with two film changes a week. Sound-on-disc was introduced in 1921. For the next few years ownership of the cinema changed to the Barger brothers, then to Mr Vivian Bennett from London, and in 1924 to Mr Stephen Green.

In 1929 Western Electric sound system was adopted. In 1937 the New Palace was run by the West of England Cinemas Ltd. During the Second World War it showed nightly performances and the occasional Saturday matinée; there was usually a change of films twice a week. The New Palace's proscenium was 33 feet in width by now, and when CinemaScope was introduced in 1955 the screen was 23½ x 14 feet. In 1958 the New Palace hosted the Welsh premier of *Carry on Sergeant* (1958), the first in the *Carry On* series of films. In the 1960s bingo was introduced one night per week. But within a further decade cinema attendances had declined and the New Palace was running a loss and was in need of refurbishment. By 1995 the balcony was regarded as being unsafe and was closed off on safety grounds. During a heavy rainstorm in November 1996, the building had to be evacuated when water got into the electrics. Also, a fire station occupied

The New Palace Cinema

The entrance to the New Palace Cinema in the 1950s

The entrance to the cinema today

The New Palace's interior before conversion

Another view of the auditorium in the early 1950s

The auditorium of the larger cinema
(© Peter Davies, Cinema Treasures)

Screens 1 and 2 of the Palace Cinema today

the adjacent building, and often the fire alarm drowned out the sound in the cinema as the fire engines were called out.

So, in 1996, the cinema closed for urgent repairs and did not reopen until 24 May 1998. It was now known as the **Palace Cinema**. New seating was installed, reducing the capacity to 538. The projection box was re-equipped. But in 1999 the cinema closed once more when the new owners, Port Talbot Plaza Cinema, went into receivership. In August 2003 the Palace was given CADW Grade II listing, and was taken over by the operators of the Coliseum Cinema in Brecon. The cinema was again renovated and a second screen was added in an empty space in the building. New Sony 4K digital projectors were installed for both screens. The circle area of the cinema is still not in use and the Palace nowadays has a seating capacity of 362 and 150 seats. It's open Tuesday to Saturday.

The **County Theatre** or **Super Cinema**, as it was originally known, on Riverside, was built in 1934 and opened a year later. The 1,000-seat venue was built for the Lewis family company, West of England Cinemas Ltd. The County's proscenium was 35 feet in width, with a stage depth of 28 feet. It also had ten dressing rooms. The theatre was equipped with Kalee projectors and a Western Electric sound system. The County was an outstanding building architecturally, with its entrance between two shops. The foyer was directly under the balcony with stairs going up on both sides. Two boxes for patrons were situated on either side of the stage. During the Second World War both films and live revues took place and the County Theatre became a popular entertainment venue for the airmen based at nearby Withybush Aerodrome. Throughout the 1950s and 1960s the County showed films mostly, but continued its traditional pantomimes during Christmas time. By the 1970s cinema attendances had declined and both the County and Palace were losing money. So the County closed in 1976 and remained empty, apart from the shop at the front and a billiard hall in the basement. In 1980

Haverfordwest's premier cinema was the County Theatre

The entrance to the County Theatre in the 1950s

The County Theatre staged a number of live shows – note the stage section

A drawing made of the County Theatre by an employee

Today apartments have been built on the site

67

the building was demolished to make way for the Riverside apartments.

The **Cinema de Luxe** was originally located in the Temperance Hall (built in 1889) in St Mary's Street. The cinema was acquired by Mr Sidney White on his return to the town in 1920. The venue had a seating capacity of around 900. The interior had a semicircle gallery where the projectors were installed. There were two shows, Monday to Saturday, with a programme change twice a week. Projection equipment was believed to be Kalee, with a Sound-on-disc system as well. Mr R.G. Noot took over Cinema de Luxe in 1928.

The **Merlin Theatre**, on Pembrokeshire College's campus, is a 240-plus-seat theatre equipped with digital projectors. It is mostly used for live performances, and Haverfordwest Film Society uses the venue for special screenings.

In 2013 the local Chamber of Commerce proposed redeveloping the land adjacent to Morrisons supermarket roundabout and Wilko stores with a multiplex cinema, shops

and restaurants. As expected, there was an objection from the owners of the Palace Cinema and the plan has been shelved.

The Temperance Hall was the site of Sidney White's Cinema de Luxe

Kidwelly, Carmarthenshire

Kidwelly (Cydweli in Welsh) lies seven miles from Llanelli. It grew to prominence during Norman times when an elaborate castle, which still stands to this day, was built. The town continued to expand during the Industrial Revolution.

The first venue used for films was the Town Hall, which was built in 1888. The hall was often a place for entertainment, including concerts by visiting variety groups. The first animated photographs were shown by Bioscope entrepreneur Mr Haydn Williams during a concert in 1901. Further Bioscope film shows followed. For the next few years there were regular visits by the travelling film showmen during the annual fairs and festivals.

The **Kidwelly Cinema**, Causeway Street, was the only purpose-built cinema in the town. The 300-seat cinema opened in 1936. It had an 18-foot-wide proscenium and a

Kidwelly's cinema in the 1950s

The empty building in the 1980s

Kidwelly's cinema has been utilised as a commercial premises for several years

stage depth of seven feet, with two reasonably-sized dressing rooms. A British Acoustic sound system was initially installed but was replaced in the early 1950s by RCA Photophone equipment. There was one show nightly, with a matinée on Saturdays and three film changes during the week. In 1947 the original owner, Mr T. Foy, sold the cinema to Mr A.R. Thomas, who remained the proprietor until its closure. Having installed CinemaScope, the addition of extra fire exits meant seating capacity was reduced to 250. Facing competition from surrounding cinemas and the restrictions imposed by the main distributors of recent films, the cinema closed for good in 1968. The building was converted into a pub in 1990 and in 2010 into retail premises.

Lampeter, Ceredigion

Lampeter (Llanbedr Pont Steffan in Welsh) is the third largest town in Ceredigion. It is also the smallest university town in Wales.

The **Victoria Hall**, Bryn Road, was opened on 23 August 1905 as assembly rooms for the community. The hall has a small balcony with the projection box situated in its middle. There is a reasonably-sized stage with dressing rooms. The hall was first listed as a cinema in 1931; it was run by the Lampeter Cinematography Company, and showed one performance nightly. The cinema was equipped with BTH Cinema projectors and sound system. It seems the cinema was only in existence until 1934, as it is not listed anywhere the following year. In the early 1950s a travelling film company visited the hall on a weekly basis for a while. In 2011 the hall was refurbished and is now run by volunteers. In 2014 the **Magic Lamp Cinema – Film Hub Wales** started, also run by volunteers.

The Victoria Hall was used for films several times a week

It is still used for the benefit of the community

Llandeilo, Carmarthenshire

Llandeilo is located on the banks of the River Towy and on the doorstep of the Brecon Beacons National Park. The town was named after the Celtic Saint Teilo.

Like most places in Wales, Llandeilo's first encounter with film was as the result of Electric Bioscope shows visiting local annual fairs.

The town's only cinema venue was on New Road. It came into existence in the 1920s. First listed in the *Kinematograph Year Book* in 1929, Mr H.W. Simonson was the proprietor. The cinema had 220 seats and a proscenium width of 20 feet, with a screen size of 14 feet. The sound system in 1931 was British Acoustic, but by 1954 it had changed to the Imperial sound system. Initially the cinema showed one film per night, with two on Saturdays and two changes of programme per week. According to the *Kinematograph Year Book* for 1947, the venue was listed as having 248 seats, with Mr H.M. Simonton [*sic*] as proprietor. The last listing was in 1954 but nowadays there are no signs of the building.

Llandovery, Carmarthenshire

Llandovery (Llanymddyfri in Welsh) is another Carmarthenshire market town situated on the River Towy. It can trace its origins back to Roman times.

Llandovery's **Public Hall**, Victoria Crescent, was registered as a cinema in 1928 and showed three films per week. The venue had 350 seats and was equipped with the Sound-on-disc system. In 1931 the sound system was changed to British Acoustic, and later changed to Kamm in 1935. The venue was known as the **Kinema** in 1935, and it showed one film nightly and two on Saturdays.

It is understood that the cinema was closed during most of the Second World War and reopened in the 1950s after a modest renovation. It changed its name to the **Castle Cinema**. The proprietor was Mr E. Taylor who was also the leaseholder of the Castle Cinema in Builth Wells. The Castle had a proscenium width of only 14 feet, the sound system was Imperial, and it could seat 230 patrons. Like most cinemas in the 1950s and 1960s it eventually closed.

Today **Llandovery Theatre**, Stone Street, shows the occasional film.

Llandysul, Ceredigion

Llandysul, a small market town in Ceredigion, dates back to the 13th century. During the English Civil War, Royalists made a stand against the Parliamentarians who were trying to cross the river there.

The **Tyssul Cinema** was operated by the Tyssul Entertainment Syndicate and showed films in the church hall between 1929 and the end of the Second World War. Films were shown every Thursday and Friday evenings, but then they became once a week events. In 1934 the cinema was listed as having Morrison sound equipment. In 1944 it belonged to the Western Cinema Circuit, with Messrs M. James and T.C. Price as proprietors. The venue had 500 seats and a 22-foot-wide proscenium. The stage was 14 feet deep, and it had two dressing rooms. It is understood that the cinema closed in the 1950s. Today Tysul Hall, built in 1955, shows the occasional film.

Llanelli, Carmarthenshire

Llanelli became a thriving industrial area due to the local coal industry. People flocked to the town seeking work from all over Wales and beyond. With a growing population, there was need for them to be entertained.

Like other areas in Wales, the first cinematograph was brought to the town by travelling showmen visiting local fairs. William Haggar came to the town with his Bioscope show in May 1910. He eventually settled in the area and set up a permanent cinema in the Royalty Theatre.

The **Royalty Theatre**, on the corner of Market Street and Water Street, had opened in 1892 and was capable of holding 1,200 people. The theatre became the town's premier venue for live performances. Fitted with most modern appliances, with a large stage and ample dressing rooms, it attracted most of the famous touring companies of the time. In 1901 the Royalty Theatre suffered serious damage due to a fire, but it was repaired and refurbished. In June 1910 the theatre was acquired by William Haggar, who obtained a cinematography licence for the building and renamed it **Haggar's Cinema**. For the next few years Haggar's Cinema put on stage shows as well as films. In the meantime, William Haggar also bought land in Cowell Street where he built his **Picture Palace**. Haggar's Cinema continued to show films until 1915 when it closed. However, in 1917 the Haggar family decided that the future was in films and cinemas, and the building was put up for sale. In June 1917 the Royalty Theatre acquired new owners and it was renamed the **Hippodrome**; it concentrated on live shows and pantomimes twice a year.

The Hippodrome's new owners were the Isaacs family who continued the tradition of two film shows per night. In 1923 Mr Harry Hunter was listed as the Hippodrome's manager at which time the venue's seating had been reduced by nearly 200 to

1,009. By 1931 Mr L.D. Abse was listed as the proprietor; a new RCA sound system was installed at this time. Glandwr Cinemas Ltd (a subsidiary of Albert Jackson Withers Cinema Circuit) took over control of the cinema in 1934 and undertook some overdue refurbishment. Sometime in 1937 the cinema closed but was reopened at Christmas for the annual pantomime. In 1940 the cinema's seating capacity was reduced further to 850 seats, as the balcony and gallery were no longer used. The cinema remained opened throughout the Second World War and performances were listed as continuous from 4.30 p.m. on weekdays and 1.30 p.m. on Saturdays, with two film changes per week. In 1954 the Hippodrome's owners were Bridgend Cinemas Ltd. CinemaScope was installed in 1955, and that gave a screen width of 30 feet. By this time seating had been reduced to 828, in the stalls only. In the mid 1960s the Hippodrome stopped showing films altogether and acquired a bingo licence

The Royalty Theatre / Haggar's Cinema in 1911. Later it was also called the Hippodrome.

The Hippodrome showed both live and film shows, but in the mid 1960s it was converted to bingo

A plaque commemorating Arthur William Haggar and the Royalty Theatre

and became known as the Argos Bingo Hall; it ceased operating in the early 1970s. The building remained empty for some years and was eventually demolished in 1977. Tesco supermarket built a new store on the site but later moved to bigger premises. The store was taken over by Tinopolis, a television production company, in the early 1990s.

The 1,000-seat **Palace Theatre**, Market Street, was built by Leon Vint as a cinema/theatre venue, initially for live variety. It opened in September 1910 – although some sources give June 1911 as the date. It was later renamed to **Vint's Electric Palace Cinema**. It remained open during the First World War, showing films and live music hall performances. In October 1923 it was taken over by Mr F.W. Carpenter, who renamed the venue the **Palace Cinema**. By 1928, Mr Harry Hunter was listed as general manager of the cinema and its operating company. With the introduction of talkies in the 1930s, a Western Electric sound system was installed. In 1934 the cinema was refurbished, and it reopened in August of that year showing three films each day with a change of programme twice a week. The Palace Cinema continued to show films throughout the Second World War. CinemaScope equipment was installed in 1955, which meant that the screen size was now 26 feet x 11 feet. In 1962 the Palace Cinema operated as a bingo and cinema venue on alternate nights. It was destroyed by fire in November 1973.

The **Athenaeum Hall**, Vaughan Street, was built in the Italian style in 1857 and was designed by Messrs Wilson and Wilcocks of Bath. Originally built as a literary and scientific institution, the 60 x 30-foot main auditorium was ideally suited for lectures and concerts. It was first used as a cinema in 1909 when John Codman of Llandudno showed his *New Empire Animated Pictures*. Soon other pioneers began using the venue for showing films. From January 1910 the venue changed its

Vint's Electric Palace Cinema in Market Street

The Athenaeum Hall was one of Llanelli's earliest venues

name to the **Picturedrome** and was leased by Mr T. Hay Samuel and managed by Mr H.B. Parkinson.

Continuous performances were scheduled from 3 p.m. every Thursday, while the rest of the week was devoted to other events. Substantial alterations took place to the building during the summer of 1910, including enlarging the stage area and installing a proper projector box. From 1914, the 550-seat Picturedrome, still under Mr H.B. Parkinson's management, showed a two-hour programme nightly on Mondays, Tuesdays, Wednesdays and Saturdays, with a change of film once a week. There was a matinée on Tuesdays and Thursdays. Often included in the programme was an organ recital by Mr Luther Owen and a guest soloist. By 1916 other cinemas had started operating in the town, and the Picturedrome closed and became a library. In 2010 major restoration work took place, turning it into a public arts and library centre.

The **Electric Theatre** was built on council-owned land alongside Old Castle Road. In the early 1900s the nearby wasteland was the site of tented Bioscope film shows. The Electric Theatre was built mainly of a wood and iron frame covered with corrugated iron sheeting. It had an ornamental façade with four candlestick-shaped pillars. The theatre opened on 4 April 1912 with a continuous film show. But, by August, the structure had collapsed and had to be rebuilt with added supports. The façade was painted white and it was renamed the **New White Cinema**, opening in August 1913 under new management (Stepney Cinemas Ltd). Towards the end of 1915 the 800-seat cinema was renamed the **Popular**. It continued to show the up-to-date silent films of the time. In 1920, Mr J. Mathias was listed as the proprietor and Mr F. Temple as manager. By then there was one nightly show, with a matinée on Saturdays and two changes of programme per week. The silent films were accompanied by a local piano player. The cinema

An aerial photo of the New White / Popular Cinema dwarfed by the Regal Cinema
(Llanelli Community Heritage website)

never converted to sound and had closed by 1929. One reason
for the closure perhaps was the larger Regal Cinema being built
next door on adjacent land. The Popular was demolished after
the Regal opened. Today the Popular Cinema site is used as a
council car park for the offices built on the site of the Regal.

The **New Dock Cinema and Playhouse** on New Dock Road
was built by Mr T. Thomas and opened in May 1913. Initially it
had seating for 1,500, mostly on benches, but this was reduced
to 800 individual seats by 1922. At the time it was felt that the
theatre had been built on the wrong side of the railway track that
separated the industrial part of Llanelli from the town centre.
The New Dock Cinema had continuous film performances as
well as live variety shows throughout the First World War and

beyond. The theatre had a proscenium width of 32 feet, with a stage depth of 14 feet. There were also three dressing rooms. The theatre closed in 1931 but reopened in July 1932 as the **Astoria Theatre** under the new management of the West of England Cinemas Ltd. During the 1930s modest alterations were done, including the installation of a Western Electric sound system and the addition of three further dressing rooms. The Astoria is not listed in any publication between 1940 and 1946 as showing continuous performances. By February 1948 it had been sold to Billy Reid and Dorothy Squires who completely renovated the building and converted it to theatre use exclusively. It was reopened in March 1950 as the **New Astoria Theatre**, and for the next few years attracted top variety acts. But it changed ownership frequently. In April 1951 the venue was sold to the Perrit brothers and 18 months later George Elrick took over the lease. The New Astoria later became famous for its lavish annual pantomimes. It closed once again, however, in 1953 and remained shut until 1954 when it was reopened and renamed the **New Dock Cinema**. By the 1960s it was used as a bingo hall and was renamed the Astoria Bingo and Social Club in September 1961. The Astoria eventually closed and the building remained empty and derelict for a number of years until it was demolished in 2008.

The **Llanelly Cinema** on Stepney Street was a purpose-built cinema which opened on Easter weekend 1911. It was owned by a newly formed company, Llanelly Cinema Ltd. The 850-seat cinema had a resident orchestra to accompany the silent films. In 1931 a British Acoustic sound system was installed and in April of that year the cinema showed Al Jolson in *The Singing Fool* (1928). In 1933 the sound system was updated to Western Electric. Throughout the Second World War the cinema continued to show performances nightly, with a matinée on Saturdays. In 1954 CinemaScope was added and, as with other

The New Astoria Theatre / New Dock Cinema prior to being demolished

cinemas in the town, admission prices increased. The cinema continued to operate until 1980 and was eventually bought by J.D. Wetherspoon after being empty for a number of years. The pub chain has refurbished it to a very high standard and kept the original cinema décor.

The **Regal Cinema**, Town Square, opened in February 1930 with the film *Show Boat* (1929) starring Laura la Plante and Joseph Schildkraut. As noted earlier, the cinema was built on land adjoining the Popular Cinema and was located near to the Town Hall. The Regal Cinema was regarded as the most luxurious and largest cinema in west Wales, and indeed the fourth largest in the whole of Wales. The 1,778-seat cinema had a café and an attached ballroom. A Western Electric sound system was installed from the outset and three shows organised daily. The Regal had a small stage and a couple of dressing rooms. The adjoining Ritz Ballroom opened in 1934. In January 1937 the Regal was taken over by Fairbank Cinemas Ltd of

The Llanelly Cinema

Its stage and screen area

84

The Llanelly Cinema is now a J.D. Wetherspoon pub

Much of the cinema's interior has been retained by the pub chain
(© J.D. Wetherspoon)

The Regal Cinema in Town Square

The Regal was next door to the Ritz Ballroom

Cardiff. They rearranged the seating and capacity was reduced to 1,500. During the Great Depression of the 1930s admission prices more or less stayed the same. The Regal continued to show films throughout the Second World War. By 1949 RCA sound system had been installed in the cinema. In September of that year Llanelli-born Dorothy Squires performed a sell-out concert there. With the installation of CinemaScope in 1956, a plan was drawn up to refurbish the building but this was not taken forward. In September 1960 the Regal ceased to show films altogether and was used as a bingo hall until it was destroyed by fire in 1969. It was eventually demolished and council offices have been built on the site. However, the Ritz next door remains open, and today it is a snooker venue, the Terry Griffiths Matchroom.

The **Odeon**, on the corner of Station Road, Lloyd Street and Mina Street, opened on 18 June 1938 with the film *Paradise for Two* (1937) starring Jack Hulbert, Patricia Ellis and Googie Withers. The 1,450-seat venue (with 900 in the stalls and 550 in the balcony) had a reasonably-sized stage and a proscenium of 40 feet in width. As was standard in most Odeons, projectors and sound equipment were supplied by BTH.

There was a film show at 2.30 p.m. every day except Sunday and three performances on a Saturday. In 1955 CinemaScope equipment was installed. By the late 1960s some Odeon cinemas were deemed unprofitable, so on 9 December 1967, 46 theatres were sold to the Classic Cinema Group, Llanelli's included. The cinema remained open under the new name of **Classic**. In the early 1970s the cinema was tripled and reopened on 1 October 1971 with Screen 1 showing Oliver Reed in *The Hunting Party* (1971); Screen 2: Franco Nero in *The Virgin and the Gipsy* (1970); and Screen 3: *Danish & Blue* (1970). The circle was extended so that Screen 1 could accommodate 516 seats. The rear stalls became screens 2 and 3, with a partitioned wall

The site of the Odeon Cinema prior to construction

The Odeon Cinema in 1947

Llanelli Odeon's auditorium, with seating for 1,450

The Odeon was acquired by the Classic Cinema Group and was tripled

The building became the Llanelli Entertainment Centre
(© *South Wales Evening Post*)

between them. Screen 2 accommodated 273 and Screen 3, 122 seats. Westar projectors were installed in the smaller cinemas. By the mid 1970s the Classic Group were selling off their cinemas however, and in May 1976 the building was bought by Llanelli Borough Council. After refurbishment and major alterations it was renamed the **Llanelli Entertainment Centre**. Lifts were installed to all floors, the stage area was improved, and there were additional dressing rooms. Screen 1 became **Theatr Elli**, capable of putting on live shows and films. The two smaller venues became Theatr 2 and 3. The Llanelli Entertainment Centre / Theatr Elli closed on 13 July 2012 prior to the opening of the new Odeon multiplex and Y Ffwrnes theatre.

On 12 October 2012 a new **Odeon Multiplex** was opened as part of the East Gate redevelopment scheme. It had been 74 years since the last Odeon cinema had opened in the town. The five-screen cinema, with seating capacity of 235, 158, 85, 76 and 58, was equipped with 3D digital projectors.

The new Odeon Multiplex cinema has five screens
(© Odeon cinemas)

Odeon Screen 5, with 58 seats

Y Ffwrnes opened in 2012 and includes a 550-seat regional theatre. It was developed by Carmarthenshire County Council as a replacement for Theatr Elli. The new culture centre contains a main auditorium which is used for live variety shows, concerts and film showing. It is equipped with digital projectors and often shows live performances from London's West End. There is also a 100-seat studio theatre, a café, a bar, as well as office space.

Llanybydder, Carmarthenshire
Llanybydder is a small market town famous for its monthly horse fair.

The **Victory Cinema** was run by Mr and Mrs M.S. Tun from 1950 to 1956. The seating capacity of the hall was 220. There were weekly film shows every Wednesday and Saturday. The projection equipment was 16 mm.

The Victory Cinema building

Machynlleth, Powys

The town of Machynlleth is famous as the location of the first national parliament of Wales called by Owain Glyndŵr in 1404.

Arthur Cheetham first showed moving pictures in the town in 1900 and used any suitable hall. Several travelling film showmen also visited the town during that time. **Powys Cinema** on Heol Powys was built in the early 1930s and was first listed as a cinema in 1935. The proprietor was Mr William Williams. The 248-seat cinema had a proscenium of 15 feet and was equipped with a Morrison sound system. The projector box was attached to the outside wall. The cinema showed two films nightly, with three changes of programme per week. In 1954 the proprietor was Mr D. Hayden Barker, and during his tenancy there was a modest refurbishment. Apartments are now located on the site.

The Powys Cinema in its heyday

Another view of the cinema showing the attached projection box

Apartments are now situated on the site of the cinema

Milford Haven, Pembrokeshire

A town once famous for its fishing industry, Milford Haven (Aberdaugleddau in Welsh) is nowadays more associated with the oil terminals in the Haven.

During its heyday in the second half of the 18th century, Henry Masterman's live theatre shows visited Milford Haven regularly. The first cinema to come to the town was Henry Wadbrook's Royal Electrograph in August 1910. Mr Wadbrook, pleased with the response and support of the town in those first few months, decided to build a permanent wooden building for his Bioscope show in Market Square. The **Wadbrook Cinema & Variety Palace** opened in December 1910. The cinema/variety format remained for the next five years. The 1912 lease of the cinema was passed to the Dooner family who renamed it **Dooner's Electric Palace**. In 1915 the epic film *1914* was shown to a packed audience. The building was destroyed by a fire in 1920 and was not rebuilt.

It is recorded that Haggar's Picture Palace visited the town in July 1911 for Milford Haven's fair.

The cinema on Robert Street was known as the **Palace** and later the **Picture Palace**. It is believed that the 275-seat cinema was built in 1913 and had a reasonably-sized stage; it held several live variety shows each year. In 1915 Mr H.J. Scard was listed as its manager. The cinema thrived during the First World War when it continued to show films and live performances. In March 1915 the film *The Enemy in Our Midst* (1914) was shown to packed houses and in May the three-part film *The Lonely House* was listed. In 1919 the cinema advertised twice nightly performances at 6.30 and 8.30. It was in the 1920s that the cinema became known as the Picture Palace. Although Sound-on-disc was introduced in 1922, it continued to employ a pianist.

H.J. Scard built three cinemas on Charles Street. The first cinema burnt down in 1919 but a second and third was built on the site, the latter eventually becoming known as the **Astoria**. The Astoria was initially a music hall, and famous stars such as comedians Sandy Powell and Jimmy James, radio presenter George Elrick, and musician Sid Millward performed there. The 729-seat auditorium had a stage depth of 19 feet and eight changing rooms to the rear and side. The proscenium was 31½ feet wide and, with the coming of CinemaScope, the screen size was 29 x 15 feet. It was equipped with Kalee projectors and a Western Electric sound system. Still in the hands of H.J. Scard in 1947, films were shown continuously, with extra performances on Saturdays.

In the 1960s cinema attendances declined substantially, so many cinema owners looked for other sources of revenue. In 1966 bingo was introduced on Wednesdays but, by the end of that decade, the cinema had closed. In October 2014 it was reopened as the Astoria bar.

The Astoria Cinema was the last of the town's cinemas to close

Since its closure the building has been used as a bingo venue and a nightclub

The **Empire Cinema** on Stratford Road, built in the early 1930s, had seating capacity for 678. It had a 32-foot proscenium and a stage depth of 20 feet, with two dressing rooms. The cinema was equipped with BTH cinema sound system. It showed films throughout the Second World War, chiefly to military personnel stationed in the town and surrounding area. In the post-war period the first live performance was the pantomime *Aladdin* in January 1946. Other live shows followed and well-known stars of the time performed there, such as comedienne Gladys Morgan.

The proprietor of the Empire was Milford Haven Cinemas Ltd. Throughout the early 1950s it showed continuous performances. Later a bingo licence was acquired, and cinema and bingo were held on different nights of the week. Eventually it was converted into a bingo hall and then into a church. The building is now up for sale.

An early photograph of the Empire Cinema
(S. Thomas)

The Empire Cinema was one of Milford Haven's most popular cinemas

The building was converted into a church

The **Torch Theatre** on St Peter's Road originally opened on 16 April 1977 but suffered financial problems within two years and was on the verge of closing. Two companies with local interests, Gulf Oil and Amoco Corporation, stepped in with sponsorship which saved the venue. In 1980 projection equipment was installed and the Torch became the only cinema in the town. A £5.4 million redevelopment took place in 2006, including the addition of the 102-seat studio theatre, a refurbished entrance and foyer, and the installation of Kinoton digital projectors in both theatres. It was reopened in March 2008 and nowadays the Torch is the most modern and well-equipped theatre in a large area of west Wales.

Today the Torch Theatre provides live performances and film shows

The Torch Theatre auditorium

Narberth, Pembrokeshire

The place-name Narberth is derived from Arberth where Pwyll, the Prince of Dyfed, presided. It's a key setting in the Welsh *Mabinogion* sagas. The town later became a Norman stronghold. Nowadays it's a popular destination for tourists.

The **Victoria Hall**, Castle Terrace, was built in 1832 as the town's market hall. It became a venue for live performances and, in 1902, animated pictures were also shown with the live shows. This arrangement, managed by William Haggar, continued until 1920. Afterwards the Victoria Hall was also used as a dance hall until sold to local brewer James Williams who used it as a bottling plant. The building was eventually sold and demolished to make way for an apartment block, Victoria Close.

The **Victoria Cinema** on the High Street opened in 1912 as a cinema/variety venue. The 300-seat auditorium had a small stage and dressing rooms, with the projection box located in the small gallery. Sound-on-disc was introduced in around 1922 but was replaced by the superior Morrison sound system before the end of that decade. It continued operating as a cinema until 1930. However, between 1933 and 1945, several refurbishments were made to the interior and the venue was totally remodelled with a new stage and sound system. Seating was reduced to 200 and this provided more legroom. It continued to show films most nights of the week throughout the Second World War. But, due to poor attendance and insufficient local support, the cinema closed for a short while in 1947 but reopened on 1 February 1948 as a theatre only, staging several well-known British pop groups, with seating increased to 400 for those shows. The hall was purchased in 1953 as a future community centre. In 1958 it was completely renovated once again and renamed the **Queens Hall**. Another refurbishment took place in 2002.

The town's only remaining cinema, the Victoria Cinema, is nowadays known as the Queens Hall

The **Grand Cinema** on Market Square was Narberth's second cinema. It opened in 1920 using the Sound-on-disc system. The cinema was owned by James Williams in partnership with the New Cinema Neyland. Initially, films were only shown on Thursday evenings. In the mid 1930s the cinema was leased to Dennis Rowlands who increased film showing to three nights per week – Thursdays, Fridays and Saturdays. The last listing of film shows at the cinema was in 1936, and it is believed that it closed a year later.

Newcastle Emlyn, Carmarthenshire

Newcastle Emlyn (Castellnewydd Emlyn in Welsh) is situated on the border of two counties, Ceredigion and Carmarthenshire. It has a 13th-century Norman castle.

The **Cawdor Hall**, built in 1892 as the town's market hall, was used extensively for entertainment. In 1913 it showed films by touring companies to audiences sat mainly on wooden benches. According to some reports a Mr J.R. Parkinson, an engineer from Ipswich, showed films at Cawdor Hall until he was granted a lease on Central Hall. In 1973 the upper room of Cawdor Hall was made into a theatre and used by a local drama group; it became known as Theatr y Daffodil. This Grade II-listed building was renovated and repaired in 2012. The Attic Players showed classic films at the venue for a short period.

The **Central Hall (Old Hall Cinema**) in Market Street was purposely built as a cinema by Mr J.R. Parkinson. It was opened in 1916 both as a cinema and public hall. It had a brick-built projection box in the gallery, a stage, and a few dressing rooms. The auditorium had seating capacity for 525 persons: 450 in the stalls and 75 in the small gallery. Electric was supplied courtesy of a water wheel turning a dynamo located on the nearby River Teifi. Talkies were introduced in 1921, firstly on disc but later by a Western Electric sound system. In 1945 the cinema closed but, between 1950 and 1952, James Rees acquired the premises to show films until the opening of the Castle Cinema. Central Hall remained empty until 1961 when it was renovated for use by the community. By 2010, however, it got into a state of disrepair. At the time of writing, a part of the building was being used by a local dance company while the rest of the building was out of bounds.

The **Castle Cinema**, New Road, opened on 20 March 1954 under the ownership of the aforementioned James Rees. The 450-seat auditorium was on one level and it had a small stage. It is believed that the projection equipment and sound system was moved from Central Hall, Rees's previous venue, but CinemaScope was installed there from the beginning. The Castle showed films four nights a week, Tuesdays, Wednesdays,

The Castle Cinema, New Road

The Castle Cinema building after it closed
(© Ken Taylor)

Fridays and Saturdays at 7.30, with the occasional matinée on Saturdays. There was a choice of two films per week. As noted earlier, by the mid 1960s cinema attendances in general had declined and, by October 1966, only two performances per week took place at the Castle, on Wednesdays and Saturdays, with two different films being shown. The venue was considered for bingo and other entertainments, but closed eventually in October 1967. The building was later taken over by a builders' merchant. Today it remains empty and is up for sale.

New Quay, Ceredigion

New Quay (Ceinewydd in Welsh) is a popular seaside resort situated on Cardigan Bay between Aberaeron and Aberporth.

The **Memorial Hall**, Towyn Road, was built in 1925 in memory of the fallen of the First World War. It was first used as a cinema in the 1930s when showmen visited the town with their films once a week during the summer season. The hall was first listed as a cinema in the *Kinematograph Year Book* in 1947. It was equipped with BTH cinema projectors and sound system. The hall had a small balcony where the projector box was located. The proscenium was 24 feet and the screen size 18 x 12 feet. The auditorium could accommodate 350 people. The stalls had removable seats, while the balcony had tip-up seats. After the Second World War there was only one show nightly, Tuesday to Friday, Easter to October, with two changes of film during the week. In 1954 the proprietor was David C. Lloyd of Aberaeron when CinemaScope was installed. By 1966 the licensee was Mr J.L. Briddon. The cinema continued to operate until 1991. Today the hall has been refurbished as a multipurpose hall and has seating capacity for 200. It still shows the occasional film. The venue nowadays is run by a team of dedicated volunteers who have extensively redeveloped by installing Cineworld and

The Memorial Hall was first listed as a cinema in 1947

The hall's auditorium

The Memorial Hall's stage and screen area
(Welsh Cinema Photo History Facebook page)

The Memorial Hall projectors in the 1970s
(Welsh Cinema Photo History Facebook page)

The hall has been renovated both inside and out

Reel Cinema projectors and sound system. The Memorial Hall played a prominent part in the film *The Edge of Love* (2008) based on Dylan Thomas's visit to New Quay in the 1960s.

Neyland, Pembrokeshire

Neyland is situated upstream from Milford Haven on the banks of the River Cleddau. In the 19th century it was a transatlantic terminal for the largest ships of the time.

As with most towns in Wales, the earliest film shows were courtesy of the travelling showmen and their electric Bioscope films. The town's only venue, owned by Mr James Williams and built in the 1920s, was the **New Cinema** on St Clements Road. In 1928 it was listed as showing films on Mondays, Tuesdays,

Fridays and Saturdays. Its manager was Mr A. McLean. It seems the cinema closed during the Second World War, as the next listing in the *Kinematograph Year Book* is in 1954. After renovation it was renamed the **Plaza**, the proprietor being Mr Harry Scard. The cinema had 324 seats, with Western Electric projectors and sound system. There was one show daily and two on Saturdays, with two changes of film per week. By all accounts the cinema closed in the 1960s and was converted into a bingo hall, but that also ceased operation. In 1972 the building was destroyed by a fire and was demolished. Today the town library stands more or less on the site.

Pembroke, Pembrokeshire
Pembroke (Penfro in Welsh) is famous for its well-preserved castle which was the birthplace of Henry Tudor, later Henry VII of England.

There was a licensed theatre in Pembroke around 1787 and there Henry Masterman and his strolling players regularly played at various venues during their winter tours. After Masterman's death in 1803, Charles Sanders took over the strolling players and made annual visits to the town. Pembroke Town Hall was often reported as hosting theatrical entertainment in the 1800s.

The first purpose-built venue for cinema/variety was **Haggar's Cinema** on Main Street. William Haggar had often visited the town with his Royal Electric Bioscope, especially during the town's Michaelmas fairs. Haggar was one of Wales's greatest cinema pioneers, making his own films and setting up cinemas throughout south Wales. His cinema occupied part of the town's Assembly Rooms. It had a proscenium of 18 feet, with a stage area of 18 feet wide by 8 feet deep. There was one dressing room at the rear. The **Pembroke Cinema**, as it was also known, opened after the First World War and had seating capacity for 300 patrons. The cinema remained in the family,

William Haggar's Cinema

Crowds waiting to enter
the cinema in the 1950s
(© Pembroke Story website)

The cinema's interior showing the screen area
(© Pembroke Story website)

The original cinema entrance became a gift shop; the entrance to the cinema was to the side

Today Haggar's Cinema has been converted into the Paddles Nightclub

with son Len Haggar taking over in 1939. During the 1930s it had been enlarged to accommodate a ballroom and a café. The cinema was equipped with RCA sound system. In 1947 it was advertised as staging one show every night with two on Saturdays. CinemaScope was installed in 1955. In the 1980s the upper floor was converted into a bingo hall, while the ground floor became a 277-seat cinema. Cinema attendances eventually declined and Haggar's Fleapit, as it was also affectionately known, closed in 1982. Today it is now the Paddles Nightclub.

Pembroke Dock, Pembrokeshire

Pembroke Dock (Doc Penfro in Welsh) can trace its existence back to Viking times. Situated on the north bank of the River Cleddau, it was originally called Paterchurch. It grew to prominence in the 19th century as a result of shipbuilding and the location of a Royal Navy dockyard in the vicinity. During the Second World War a Sunderland flying boat station was located in the town.

Pembroke Dock, with its military connections, could boast a number of entertainment venues over the years. Several touring variety groups visited the town performing in such places as the Town Hall, Market Hall, Ord's Theatre, Temperance Hall and the Queens Theatre. The first licensed theatre in the town dates from 1788.

The **Grand Cinema**, Meyrick Street, was opened in 1914 as a cinema/variety venue. It was a timber-framed building clad in corrugated iron sheeting, while the front was rendered brickwork with two entrances. There was a small stage and a room at the rear which could be used as a dressing room. During the silent era, films were accompanied by a piano. The proscenium opening was 32 feet wide and, when CinemaScope was introduced in the 1950s, the 32 x 12-foot screen occupied the whole proscenium. The cinema seating capacity was 550 but this was reduced to 420 with the introduction of CinemaScope. Back in 1924 two shows per night were advertised, with two changes of film per week. However, by 1951, only one performance a night and a matinée on Saturday afternoons was publicised. As a result of the downturn in cinema attendances, the Grand closed in 1974. In 1980 the building was demolished. Today the site is occupied by St Govan's Shopping Centre.

The **Queen's Theatre** opened in 1905 as a variety venue. It was equipped with a reasonably-sized stage and had dressing rooms at the rear. Several well-known performers of the period, such as Will Euston, Ella and Edward, Ivy Rocheford and Barney Deely appeared there. By 1911 the theatre was in financial difficulties, so a year later it invested in projection equipment and began showing films. Sound equipment was introduced in

The Grand Cinema was demolished in 1980

1922 and by 1929 the Queen's Theatre was exclusively a cinema. The cinema closed during the Second World War and was used as a government warehouse.

The **Picture Palace**, Queen Street, opened in 1910 as **White's Palace** cinema/variety hall. As was common at that time, variety acts performed between film shows. In 1914 the venue was taken over by new owner and manager Tom Barger, who renamed it **Barger's Picture Palace**. He introduced variety and film shows on alternate weeks, and apparently the live shows were actually more popular than the films. In 1921 there was a major rebuilding of the theatre – the auditorium was enlarged with a new stage and projection box. It was now advertised as the **New Palace**. The following year the Palace was for sale but failed to sell in an auction on 20 July 1922. In 1923 it was reopened as a cinema,

The Picture Palace became Palace Bingo

with Tom Barger still as manager. By now two Kalee sound projectors had been installed. It remained open until 1940 but during most of the Second World War it was used to store aircraft alloy. It reopened as a cinema in 1947/8, showing one performance per night. The cinema closed in 1960 to reopen as a bingo hall run by Top Ten Bingo Club. The bingo hall closed in March 2013 and the building remains empty.

The **Garrison Theatre / Astra Cinema** was initially built by the Admiralty as a garrison chapel in 1830. When the dockyard closed in 1926 the chapel continued to be used for a while. But when the Army left in 1930 the chapel was converted into a theatre/cinema equipped with a stage and a projector box built on the balcony situated above the entrance. Two BTH cinema projectors and associate sound systems were installed. Throughout the Second World War the theatre showed both films and live variety shows. When the Sunderland flying boat station closed in 1957, the theatre was converted into a motor museum. That, however, closed too in 1975 and the building became derelict. Since then the Grade II-listed building has been in the process of being restored.

The Garrison Theatre / Astra Cinema
(© W.O. Trevor Mills)

Pontarddulais, County of Swansea

Pontarddulais is a town situated some ten miles north-west of the city of Swansea. Noted for its industrial heritage, its male voice choir is renowned throughout Wales and beyond.

As with most towns in Wales, the first glimpse of entertainment, especially film, was due to the travelling electric film shows, such as Walter Haggar's. Towards the end of the 1900s however, roller-skating had been introduced to the country and a roller rink was built in the town. This was also used as a concert hall. In 1910 Walter Haggar took over this building and within a year began showing films. It soon became known as the **Cinema**, later the **Picture Hall**, and eventually the **Picturedrome**. As was the norm at the time, the film shows commenced with a variety

The roller-skating rink / Picturedrome

show or a choral concert. One show per night was scheduled Monday to Saturday. The Picturedrome came under the control of W. Haggar Jnr in 1920. In 1924 it was wrecked by fire.

At the beginning of the 1920s the Pryce family took out a lease on the local Temperance Hall, renaming it the **Gym Cinema**. They began showing films, but within five years the cinema had closed.

On 13 September 1924 another new cinema was opened, the **Tivoli** on St Teilo Street, by the company Tivoli (Pontarddulais) Ltd – the major shareholder being Mr Max Corne. The 768-seat cinema had a proscenium of 30 feet and a screen size of 28 x 14 feet. Electricity was generated on the premises by a diesel generator housed in a building at the rear. There was also a small stage for live entertainment. The projectors were Western Electric Westairs and the sound equipment was from Clark and Company. The Tivoli continued to show films throughout the Second World War,

The Tivoli Cinema in the 1980s
(Cinema Treasures website)

with one show daily Monday to Friday and occasionally two on Saturdays. There were two programme changes per week. After the war people began travelling further afield for entertainment, as some Swansea cinemas blocked some new films from being shown in outlying areas such as Pontarddulais. The CinemaScope system was later fitted but attendances declined and the cinema closed in the 1960s. The derelict building was finally demolished in 1990.

According to the *Kinematograph Year Book* another cinema, the **Memorial and Welfare Hall**, operated from 1959 into the 1970s. It had some 700 seats. The cinema had a 28-foot-wide CinemaScope screen and showed one performance nightly. However, it too closed as people preferred to travel to Swansea which had a greater choice of films to see. But, according to local historians, the Memorial and Welfare Hall and the Tivoli were one and the same, and were referred to in the *Kinematograph Year Books* under different names. The

Memorial and Welfare Hall finally closed for good in 1980 and remained derelict for ten years until it was, as noted, demolished in 1990.

Tenby, Pembrokeshire

Tenby (Dinbych-y-pysgod in Welsh), on the south Pembrokeshire coast, has been a popular seaside resort since the 19th century and has had a number of entertainment venues. Nowadays, however, they are few and far between.

In the early days of cinematography, the seaside resorts attracted a number of the early moving pictures' pioneers. Music halls also sprang up and some eventually became cinemas. In Tenby there were the Assembly Rooms adjoining the Marine Baths on Frog Street, the Royal Gate House Hotel Assembly Rooms, the Public Hall, the Temperance Hall and the De Valence Pavilion.

In 1902/3 William Haggar's Royal Electric Bioscope shows appeared at Tenby's annual St Margaret's fair. Dooner, Crecraft and Wadbrook travelling film shows also visited Tenby.

The **Public Hall** on Warren Street, a variety music hall, was the first to show animated films. In 1901, Mr Fredrick Dale and his Bioscope showed *The Royal Funeral Procession (Queen Victoria)* and *The State Opening of Parliament* for one night. More films were also shown later that year at the venue.

The first cinema to abide by the new rules of the Cinematograph Act of 1909 was the purpose-built venue in Coronation Gardens. The garden's proprietor, Mr F.B. Mason, was granted a licence in 1910. As most of the venue was in the open air, the projector box was located behind a privet hedge. The cinema only operated during the summer months – provided it did not rain – and it seems that it ceased to exist after 1913.

Tenby's first permanent cinema was at the **Assembly Rooms** which belonged to the Royal Gate House Hotel. It started operating in 1911. By 1913 it had changed its name to the **Royal Assembly Rooms**. The **Central Hall**, Lower Frog Street, was also granted a licence as a cinema after minor alterations had been made to the building. Renamed as the **Tenby Electric Cinema**, it opened for the first time on 26 August 1912. The proprietors were Messrs Harry and Sidney Thomas. The cinema showed films Monday to Saturday (one show per night, with two on Saturdays) and there was a film change twice a week. Later, the Thomas brothers took over the Royal Assembly Rooms and, after renovation, it reopened on 13 April 1914 as the **Picture House**. The theatre/cinema had a proscenium of 35 feet and a stage depth of 35 feet and also two dressing rooms. The Picture House showed one performance nightly, Monday to Friday, and two on Saturdays.

In 1924 a new luxury cinema, **Super Cinema**, was built in Warren Street. It was owned by B. and A.G. Beynon. The building was 80 feet in length, 34 feet wide and was 22 feet high. The main entrance faced the Manse Gardens. There was a balcony over the entrance where the projection box was located. The cinema had 450 tip-up seats covered in red velvet. Opening night was on 21 April 1924, with the film *Bella Donna* (1923) shown for three nights. Two years later the cinema was leased by Mr M.W. Shanly who invested a large amount of money in renovating it – murals and ceiling decorations made by local artist Reginald Morris were added. It reopened on 1 November 1930 with Western Electric sound system. The Super Cinema was sold to Messrs Phillips in July 1937 and became the **Super Theatre**, home to a repertory company until 1939. During the Second World War it was taken over by the military and used as a Navy, Army and Air Force Institute for servicemen based in the town. In 1946 the cinema was acquired by the Milford Haven Cinema Company. It was renamed **Little Theatre**, and held live variety shows during the summer months. It closed in 1956 and eventually became an amusement arcade. Since then it has been converted into apartments.

The **De Valence Pavilion**, Upper Frog Street, was built in 1928 as a theatre and cinema. It had moveable seating capacity for nearly 600, and the general purpose building had a stage and six dressing rooms. The De Valence Pavilion had Western Electric sound system fitted in 1932. The venue was closed in 1939 and used by the military authorities. Films were shown on Sundays only to military personnel based in Tenby. After the Second World War the De Valance Pavilion ceased to be a cinema but was used as a dance hall. In 1970 the pavilion was demolished and a new building erected with a stage measuring 24 x 24 feet and removable seating at the rear and a bar and restaurant. In 2010 it closed and awaits a buyer.

The **Royal Assembly Rooms / Picture House**, White Lion Street, was built in 1913 and renovated and enlarged in 1928 to incorporate a dance hall. It reopened on 16 July 1928 and was called the **Royal Playhouse Cinema**. Early films shown were *Good Morning, Judge* (1928) and *The Call of the Heart* (1928). In the 1930s Western Electric sound system was installed. The Playhouse had a seating capacity of 700, a proscenium of 35 feet with a screen size of 17 x 14 feet. There were two reasonably-sized dressing rooms at the rear of the building. Run by Mr E.A. Parker, it showed films twice nightly, Monday to Saturday. With the outbreak of the Second World War in 1939, the cinema closed for a short time but was allowed to reopen. At the end of the war Gatehouse Estates took over the Playhouse. By 1947 the Royal Playhouse was advertising continuous performances starting at 4.30 p.m. Monday to Friday and from 2 p.m. on Saturdays. CinemaScope was installed in 1955 which increased the screen size to 29 feet x 16 feet, but also enhanced the prices! By then performances had been reduced to one per night with

The Royal Playhouse was a popular cinema in the town
(© Ceridwen)

two on Saturdays. In the 1980s the Playhouse was taken over by Fry's Enterprise Ltd who reduced the seating to 540 by fitting more comfortable seats. For the next few years the Playhouse continued to show films and some live performances but, in January 2011, it closed for good. The listed building remained empty awaiting a buyer and developer. It was eventually partly demolished and rebuilt as a retail unit, but the old façade was retained. Today it is a Poundland store.

Shanly's Amusement Pavilion / South Beach Pavilion was a six-storey entertainment centre built on the South Beach overlooking St Catherine's Island. It contained a cinema, dance hall, roof gardens, skating rink, amusement arcades, a restaurant and a number of confectionary booths and shops. The 660-seat cinema opened on 12 July 1929 with three shows daily. Its proscenium was 25 feet, with a stage depth of 12 feet. The screen

Shanly's Amusement Pavilion / South Beach Pavilion
(Cinema Treasures website)

An aerial view of the Shanly's Amusement Pavilion
(Cinema Treasures website)

size was 24 x 14 feet. There were two dressing rooms at the rear. In 1930 it was equipped with Western Electric sound system. In 1938 Shanly's Pavilion became the first cinema in town to be equipped with a Hammond LaFleur organ. It remained open throughout the Second World War.

CinemaScope was introduced in 1954 but management did not increase ticket prices as had happened at the Playhouse. From 1966 onwards the cinema closed during the winter months, leaving just the amusement arcade and café open. In early 1975 Shanly's Pavilion closed for good and was demolished in 1978.

Tywyn, Gwynedd

Tywyn is a seaside resort on Cardigan Bay and is a terminus for the Talyllyn Railway.

Tywyn's **Assembly Rooms** on Corbett Square opened in 1893 for the community to use for dances, variety shows and local events. Films were first shown in the hall by Arthur Cheetham and William Haggar during their tours of the area in the early 1900s. The Assembly Rooms were first listed as a cinema in 1947, and known as the **Tywyn Cinema**. Equipped with BTH Supa Cinema Mk2 35 / 16 mm projectors, CinemaScope was introduced in 1955 which gave a 31-foot screen. Initially the cinema had seating for 630 but this was reduced 425 seats. Continuous film shows were available Monday to Saturday, with a matinée performance as well on Saturdays. In 1955 there were three film changes during the week.

By 1966 the proprietor was Mr H.T. Parkes of Prestatyn. The cinema changed its name in the 1970s to the **Talking Cinema** and it was operated by Sidelines Production. Known once more as the Tywyn Cinema in 1990, it changed its name to the **Magic Lantern Cinema** in 2012. In 2000 the cinema was

Towyn. Assembly Room and Corbett & Raven Hotel.

An old postcard showing the Assembly Rooms

Tywyn's cinema as it is today

refurbished and redecorated, and a bar was incorporated into the foyer. Seating was reduced to 368 and new state-of-the-art 3D projectors with 7.1 Surround Sound installed in March 2013 (although the BTH projectors were kept for showing older films). In 2010 Mark Bond and Geoff Hill took out a lease on the cinema and it has now made it onto the UK's best independent cinema list. Today it is renowned for its artistic murals painted on the auditorium walls.

Tywyn's other public building, **Neuadd y Pentre** (Village Hall), Brook Street, was built in 1912 and used as a Territorial Army Drill Hall. But it was also used occasionally as a cinema in the 1920s, mostly by visiting film showmen. Today it is used as a community hall and has a Wurlitzer organ on the stage.

The Magic Lantern Cinema's entrance

Its auditorium

Artistic murals painted on the auditorium walls
(© Magic Lantern Cinema)

127

Acknowledgements

Special thanks to:

Roger Ebert of the *cinematreasures.org* website and all its contributors
Brian Hornsey, for his vast knowledge of cinemas in this country
arthurlloyd.co.uk
British Independent Cinemas Association
Carmarthenshire Archives and Carmarthenshire County Museum
Ceredigion Archives
Ceredigion Museum
Coflein
Cross Hands Public Hall and Cinema
Gwynedd Archives
Haverfordwest Library and Information Centre
Kinematograph Magazine and *Year Books*
Llanelli Library
The Mercia Cinema Society
The National Science and Media Museum, Bradford
The National Library of Wales, Aberystwyth
overthefootlights.co.uk
Pembrokeshire Archives
Pembroke Story website
Save the Old Llanelli Odeon Facebook page
Silver Screen Archives
South Wales Evening Post
walesonline.co.uk
Welsh Cinema Photo History Facebook page
J.D. Wetherspoon

Also many thanks to various individuals, past projectionists and managers who worked in the cinemas and have contributed valuable information and photographs.

Selected Bibliography

Berry, David, *Wales and Cinema: The First One Hundred Years*, University of Wales Press (1995).

Hornsey, Brian, *Cinemas of Wales*, Mercia Cinema Society (1996).

Hornsey, Brian, *Ninety Years of Cinemas in Carmarthen*, Mercia Cinema Society (1997).

Hornsey, Brian, *Ninety Years of Cinemas in Llanelli*, Mercia Cinema Society (1995).

Thomas, Beth, *Cytiau Chwain a Phalasau Breuddwydion / Fleapits and Picture Palaces*,